GENTLE

and

LOWLY

Journal

Dane Ortlund

WHEATON, ILLINOIS

Gentle and Lowly Journal

Copyright © 2021 by Dane Ortlund

Published by Crossway

1300 Crescent Street

Wheaton, Illinois 60187

Cover design: Jordan Singer

First printing 2021

Printed in the United States of America

Trade paperback ISBN: 978-1-4335-8038-3

Crossway is a publishing ministry of Good News Publishers.

LSC	31	30	29	28	27	26	25	24	23	22	21
12	11	10	9	8	7	6	5	4	3	2	1

Introduction

DANE ORTLUND

Great truths are not meant to be hurriedly absorbed or quickly downloaded. They are meant to be slowly digested. Pondered slowly, reflectively, and thereby taken way down deep into our hearts to stay. That is the purpose of the *Gentle and Lowly Journal*.

Each of the twenty-three sections of this journal correspond to the twenty-three chapters of *Gentle and Lowly: The Heart of Christ for Sinners and Sufferers*. For each section of this journal, reflecting each chapter of that book, a key Bible text has been paired with a historical reflection from a great theologian of the past, along with an excerpt from the book.

These brief selections are intended to foster reflection and prayer as readers consider the depths of Christ's great heart for them *in* their sins and their sufferings—not once they get on the other side of these adversities. Space is provided to record your own meditations and reflections as you ponder the Lord Jesus yourself.

May this journal take your own heart deep into his heart—he who is, most deeply—wonder of wonders—"gentle and lowly in heart" (Matt. 11:29).

1 His Very Heart

Come to me, all who labor and are heavy laden, and I will give you rest. Take my yoke upon you, and learn from me, for I am gentle and lowly in heart, and you will find rest for your souls. For my yoke is easy, and my burden is light.

MATTHEW 11:28–30

Men are apt to have contrary conceits of Christ, but he tells them his disposition there, by preventing such hard thoughts of him, to allure them unto him the more. We are apt to think that he, being so holy, is therefore of a severe and sour disposition against sinners, and not able to bear them. "No," says he; "I am meek; gentleness is my nature and temper."

THOMAS GOODWIN

We learn much in the four Gospels about Christ's teaching. We read of his birth, his ministry, and his disciples. We are told of his travels and prayer habits. We find lengthy speeches and repeated objections by his hearers, prompting further teaching. We learn of the way he understood himself to fulfill the whole Old Testament. And we learn in all four accounts of his unjust arrest and shameful death and astonishing resurrection. . . . But in only one place—perhaps the most wonderful words ever uttered by human lips—do we hear Jesus himself open up to us his very heart (Matt. 11:28–30). In the one place in the Bible where the Son of God pulls back the veil and lets us peer way down into the core of who he is, we are not told that he is "austere and demanding in heart." We are not told that he is "exalted and dignified in heart." We are not even told that he is "joyful and generous in heart." Letting Jesus set the terms, his surprising claim is that he is "gentle and lowly in heart."

DANE ORTLUND

2   His Heart in Action

Now when Jesus heard this, he withdrew from there in a boat to a desolate place by himself. But when the crowds heard it, they followed him on foot from the towns. When he went ashore he saw a great crowd, and he had compassion on them and healed their sick.

MATTHEW 14:13–14

When [Christ] saw the people in misery, his bowels yearned within him; the works of grace and mercy in Christ, they come from his bowels first. [That is,] whatsoever Christ did . . . he did it out of love, and grace, and mercy . . . he did it inwardly from his very bowels.

RICHARD SIBBES

This compassion comes in waves over and over again in Christ's ministry, driving him to heal the sick ("and he had compassion on them and healed their sick," Matt. 14:14), feed the hungry ("I have compassion on the crowd because they have been with me now three days and have nothing to eat," Matt. 15:32), teach the crowds ("and he had compassion on them . . . and he began to teach them many things," Mark 6:34), and wipe away the tears of the bereaved ("he had compassion on her and said to her, 'Do not weep,'" Luke 7:13). The Greek word for "compassion" is the same in all these texts and refers most literally to the bowels or guts of a person—it's an ancient way of referring to what rises up from one's innermost core. This compassion reflects the deepest heart of Christ.

DANE ORTLUND

3   The Happiness of Christ

For the joy that was set before him endured the cross, despising the shame, and is seated at the right hand of the throne of God.

HEBREWS 12:2

[The] glory and happiness of Christ [are] enlarged and increased still, as his members come to have the purchase of his death more and more laid forth upon them; so as when their sins are pardoned, their hearts more sanctified, and their spirits comforted, then comes he to see the fruit of his labor, and is comforted thereby, for he is the more glorified by it, yea, he is much more pleased and rejoiced in this than themselves can be. And this keeps up in his heart his care and love unto his children here below, to water and refresh them every moment.

THOMAS GOODWIN

We tend to think that when we approach Jesus for help in our need and mercy amid our sins, we somehow detract from him, lessen him, impoverish him. Goodwin argues otherwise. Jesus surprises us in "exercising acts of grace, and from his continual doing good unto and for his members . . . from his filling them with all mercy, grace, comfort, and felicity, himself becoming yet more full, by filling them." As truly God, Christ cannot become any more full; he shares in his Father's immortal, eternal, unchangeable fullness. Yet as truly man, Christ's heart is not drained by our coming to him; his heart is filled up all the more by our coming to him. To put it the other way around: when we hold back, lurking in the shadows, fearful and failing, we miss out not only on our own increased comfort but on Christ's increased comfort. He lives for this. This is what he loves to do. His joy and ours rise and fall together. Jesus Christ is comforted when you draw from the riches of his atoning work, because his own body is getting healed.

DANE ORTLUND

4   Able to Sympathize

Since then we have a great high priest who has passed through the heavens, Jesus, the Son of God, let us hold fast our confession. For we do not have a high priest who is unable to sympathize with our weaknesses, but one who in every respect has been tempted as we are, yet without sin. Let us then with confidence draw near to the throne of grace, that we may receive mercy and find grace to help in time of need.

HEBREWS 4:14–16

I have chosen this text [Heb. 4:15], as that which above any other speaks his heart most, and sets out the frame and workings of it towards sinners; and that so sensibly that it does, as it were, take our hands, and lay them upon Christ's breast, and let us feel how his heart beats and his affections yearn toward us, even now he is in glory—the very scope of these words being manifestly to encourage believers against all that may discourage them, from the consideration of Christ's heart toward them now in heaven.

THOMAS GOODWIN

The reason that Jesus is in such close solidarity with us is that the difficult path we are on is not unique to us. He has journeyed on it himself. It is not only that Jesus can relieve us from our troubles, like a doctor prescribing medicine; it is also that, before any relief comes, he is with us in our troubles, like a doctor who has endured the same disease. Jesus is not Zeus. He was a sinless man, not a sinless Superman. He came as a normal man to normal men. He knows what it is to be thirsty, hungry, despised, rejected, scorned, shamed, embarrassed, abandoned, misunderstood, falsely accused, suffocated, tortured, and killed. He knows what it is to be lonely. His friends abandoned him when he needed them most; had he lived today, every last Twitter follower and Facebook friend would have un-friended him when he turned thirty-three—he who will never un-friend us.

DANE ORTLUND

5 He Can Deal Gently

He can deal gently with the ignorant and wayward.

HEBREWS 5:2

[Jesus, our high priest, can] no more cast off poor sinners for their ignorance and wanderings than a nursing father should cast away a sucking child for its crying. . . . Thus ought it to be with a high priest, and thus is it with Jesus Christ. He is able, with all meekness and gentleness, with patience and moderation, to bear with the infirmities, sins, and provocations of his people, even as a nurse or a nursing father bears with the weakness . . . of a poor infant.

JOHN OWEN

When we sin, we are encouraged to bring our mess to Jesus because he will know just how to receive us. He doesn't handle us roughly. He doesn't scowl and scold. He doesn't lash out, the way many of our parents did. And all this restraint on his part is not because he has a diluted view of our sinfulness. He knows our sinfulness far more deeply than we do. Indeed, we are aware of just the tip of the iceberg of our depravity, even in our most searching moments of self-knowledge. His restraint simply flows from his tender heart for his people. Hebrews is not just telling us that instead of scolding us, Jesus loves us. It's telling us the kind of love he has: rather than dispensing grace to us from on high, he gets down with us, he puts his arm around us, he deals with us in the way that is just what we need. He deals gently with us.

DANE ORTLUND

6   I Will Never Cast Out

All that the Father giveth me shall come to me; and him that cometh to me I will in no wise cast out.

JOHN 6:37, KJV

But I am a great sinner, say you.

"I will in no wise cast out," says Christ.

But I am a backsliding sinner, say you.

"I will in no wise cast out," says Christ.

But I have sinned against light, say you.

"I will in no wise cast out," says Christ.

But I have no good thing to bring with me, say you.

"I will in no wise cast out," says Christ.

JOHN BUNYAN, LANGUAGE LIGHTLY UPDATED

What is most deeply instinctive to [Christ] as our sins and sufferings pile up? What keeps him from growing cold? The answer is, his heart. The atoning work of the Son, decreed by the Father and applied by the Spirit, ensures that we are safe eternally. But a text such as John 6:37 [lit., "the one coming to me I will not—*not*—cast out"] reassures us that this is not only a matter of divine decree but divine desire. This is heaven's delight. Come to me, says Christ. I will embrace you into my deepest being and never let you go. Have you considered what is true of you if you are in Christ? In order for you to fall short of loving embrace into the heart of Christ both now and into eternity, Christ himself would have to be pulled down out of heaven and put back in the grave. His death and resurrection make it just for Christ never to cast out his own, no matter how often they fall. But animating this work of Christ is the heart of Christ. He cannot bear to part with his own, even when they most deserve to be forsaken.

DANE ORTLUND

7 What Our Sins Evoke

The law came in to increase the trespass, but where sin increased, grace abounded all the more.

ROMANS 5:20

Christ takes part with you, and is so far from being provoked against you, as all his anger is turned upon your sin to ruin it; yes, his pity is increased the more towards you, even as the heart of a father is to a child that has some loathsome disease, or as one is to a member of his body that has leprosy, he hates not the member, for it is his flesh, but the disease, and that provokes him to pity the part affected the more. What shall not make for us, when our sins, that are both against Christ and us, shall be turned as motives to him to pity us the more? The greater the misery is, the more is the pity when the party is beloved. Now of all miseries, sin is the greatest; and while you look at it as such, Christ will look upon it as such also. And he, loving your persons, and hating only the sin, his hatred shall all fall, and that only upon the sin, to free you of it by its ruin and destruction, but his affections shall be the more drawn out to you; and this as much when you lie under sin as under any other affliction. Therefore fear not.

THOMAS GOODWIN

If you are part of Christ's own body, your sins evoke his deepest heart, his compassion and pity. He "takes part with you"—that is, he's on your side. He sides with you against your sin, not against you because of your sin. He hates sin. But he loves you.

DANE ORTLUND

8   To the Uttermost

He always lives to make intercession for them.

HEBREWS 7:25

[Christ] turns the Father's eyes to his own righteousness to avert his gaze from our sins. He so reconciles the Father's heart to us that by his intercession he prepares a way and access for us to the Father's throne.

JOHN CALVIN

Intercession applies what the atonement accomplished. Christ's present heavenly intercession on our behalf is a reflection of the fullness and victory and completeness of his earthly work, not a reflection of anything lacking in his earthly work. The atonement accomplished our salvation; intercession is the moment-by-moment application of that atoning work. In the past, Jesus did what he now talks about; in the present, Jesus talks about what he then did. . . . Intercession is the constant hitting "refresh" of our justification in the court of heaven. Pressing in more deeply, Christ's intercession reflects how profoundly personal our rescue is. If we knew about Christ's death and resurrection but not his intercession, we would be tempted to view our salvation in overly formulaic terms. It would feel more mechanical than is true to who Christ actually is. His interceding for us reflects his heart—the same heart that carried him through life and down into death on behalf of his people is the heart that now manifests itself in constant pleading with and reminding and prevailing upon his Father to always welcome us.

DANE ORTLUND

9 An Advocate

My little children, I am writing these things to you so that you may not sin. But if anyone does sin, we have an advocate with the Father, Jesus Christ the righteous.

1 JOHN 2:1

Christ, as Priest, goes before, and Christ, as an Advocate, comes after. Christ, as Priest, continually intercedes; Christ, as Advocate, in case of great transgressions, pleads. Christ, as Priest, has need to act always, but Christ, as Advocate, sometimes only. Christ, as Priest, acts in time of peace; but Christ, as Advocate, in times of broils, turmoils, and sharp contentions; wherefore, Christ, as Advocate, is, as I may call him, a reserve, and his time is then to arise, to stand up and plead, when his own are clothed with some filthy sin that of late they have fallen into.

JOHN BUNYAN

The Bible nowhere teaches that once we have been savingly united with Christ, we will find grievous sins to be a thing of the past. . . . And that's what Christ's advocacy is for. It's God way of encouraging us not to throw in the towel. . . . When you sin, remember your legal standing before God because of the work of Christ; but remember also your advocate before God because of the heart of Christ. He rises up and defends your cause, based on the merits of his own sufferings and death. Your salvation is not merely a matter of a saving formula, but of a saving person. When you sin, his strength of resolve rises all the higher. When his brothers and sisters fail and stumble, he advocates on their behalf *because it is who he is.* He cannot bear to leave us alone to fend for ourselves.

DANE ORTLUND

10   The Beauty of the Heart of Christ

Whoever loves father or mother more than me is not worthy of me, and whoever loves son or daughter more than me is not worthy of me.

MATTHEW 10:37

Everything that is lovely in God is in Christ, and everything that is or can be lovely in any man is in him: for he is man as well as God, and he is the holiest, meekest, most humble, and every way the most excellent man that ever was.

JONATHAN EDWARDS

Have we considered the loveliness of the heart of Christ? Perhaps beauty is not a category that comes naturally to mind when we think about Christ. Maybe we think of God and Christ in terms of truth, not beauty. But the whole reason we care about sound doctrine is for the sake of preserving God's beauty, just as the whole reason we care about effective focal lenses on a camera is to capture with precision the beauty we photograph. Let Jesus draw you in through the loveliness of his heart. This is a heart that upbraids the impenitent with all the harshness that is appropriate, yet embraces the penitent with more openness than we are able to feel. It is a heart that walks us into the bright meadow of the felt love of God. It is a heart that drew the despised and forsaken to his feet in self-abandoning hope. It is a heart of perfect balance and proportion, never overreacting, never excusing, never lashing out. It is a heart that throbs with desire for the destitute. It is a heart that floods the suffering with the deep solace of shared solidarity in that suffering. It is a heart that is gentle and lowly.

DANE ORTLUND

11 The Emotional Life of Christ

When Jesus saw her weeping, and the Jews who had come with her also weeping, he was deeply moved in his spirit and greatly troubled.

JOHN 11:33

Inextinguishable fury seizes upon [Jesus when he approached Lazarus's grave]. . . . It is death that is the object of his wrath, and behind death him who has the power of death, and whom he has come into the world to destroy. Tears of sympathy may fill his eyes, but this is incidental. His soul is held by rage. . . . The raising of Lazarus thus becomes, not an isolated marvel, but . . . a decisive instance and open symbol of Jesus' conquest of death and hell. What John does for us . . . is to uncover for us the heart of Jesus, as he wins for us our salvation. Not in cold unconcern, but in flaming wrath against the foe, Jesus smites in our behalf. He has not only saved us from the evils which oppress us; he has felt for and with us in our oppression, and under the impulse of these feelings has wrought out our redemption.

B. B. WARFIELD

While Christ is a lion to the impenitent, he is a lamb to the penitent—the reduced, the open, the hungry, the desiring, the confessing, the self-effacing. He hates with righteous hatred all that plagues you. Remember that Isaiah 53 speaks of Christ bearing our griefs and carrying our sorrows (v. 4). He wasn't only punished in our place, experiencing something we never will (condemnation); he also suffered with us, experiencing what we ourselves do (mistreatment). In your grief, he is grieved. In your distress, he is distressed.

DANE ORTLUND

12 A Tender Friend

The Son of Man came eating and drinking, and they say, "Look at him!
A glutton and a drunkard, a friend of tax collectors and sinners!"

MATTHEW 11:19

God in Christ allows such little, poor creatures as you are to come to him,
to love communion with him, and to maintain a communication of love
with him. You may go to God and tell him how you love him and open
your heart and he will accept of it. . . . He is come down from heaven and
has taken upon him the human nature in purpose, that he might be near to
you and might be, as it were, your companion.

JONATHAN EDWARDS

Though the crowds call him the friend of sinners as an indictment, the
label is one of unspeakable comfort for those who know themselves to be
sinners. That Jesus is friend to sinners is only contemptible to those who
feel themselves not to be in that category. What does it mean that Christ
is a friend to sinners? At the very least, it means that he enjoys spending
time with them. It also means that they feel welcome and comfortable
around him. Notice the passing line that starts off a series of parables in
Luke: "Now the tax collectors and sinners were all drawing near to hear
him" (Luke 15:1). The very two groups of people whom Jesus is accused
of befriending in Matthew 11 are those who can't stay away from him in
Luke 15. They are at ease around him. They sense something different
about him. Others hold them at arms' length, but Jesus offers the enticing
intrigue of fresh hope. What he is really doing, at bottom, is pulling them
into his heart.

DANE ORTLUND

13   Why the Spirit?

It is to your advantage that I go away, for if I do not go away, the Helper will not come to you. But if I go, I will send him to you.

JOHN 16:7

My father and I have but only one friend, who lies in the bosom of us both, and proceeds from us both, the Holy Ghost, and in the meantime I will send him to you. . . . He shall be a better Comforter unto you than I am to be. . . . He will comfort you better than I should do with my bodily presence. He shall tell you, if you will listen to him, and not grieve him, nothing but stories of my love. . . . All his speech in your hearts will be to advance me, and to greaten my worth and love unto you, and it will be his delight to do it.

THOMAS GOODWIN, PARAPHRASE OF JOHN 16:5–7

The Spirit regenerates us, convicts us, empowers us with gifts, testifies in our hearts that we are God's children, leads us, makes us fruitful, grants and nurtures in us resurrection life, enables us to kill sin, intercedes for us when we don't know what to pray, guides us into truth, transforms us into the image of Christ . . . [and] *causes us to actually feel Christ's heart for us.* . . . The Spirit makes the heart of Christ real to us: not just heard, but seen; not just seen, but felt; not just felt, but enjoyed. The Spirit takes what we read in the Bible and believe on paper about Jesus's heart and moves it from theory to reality, from doctrine to experience.

DANE ORTLUND

14   Father of Mercies

Blessed be the God and Father of our Lord Jesus Christ, the Father of mercies and God of all comfort.

2 CORINTHIANS 1:3

His love is not a forced love, which he strives only to bear toward us, because his Father hath commanded him to marry us; but it is his nature, his disposition. . . . This disposition is free and natural to him; he should not be God's Son else, nor take after his heavenly Father, unto whom it is natural to show mercy, but not so to punish, which is his strange work, but mercy pleases him; he is "the Father of mercies," he begets them naturally.

THOMAS GOODWIN

As Paul opens 2 Corinthians he gives us a window into what came into *his* mind when he thought about God. Yes, the Father is just and righteous. Unswervingly, unendingly. Without such a doctrine, such a reassurance, we would have no hope that all wrongs would one day be righted. But what is his heart? What flows out from his deepest being? What does he beget? Mercies. He is the Father of mercies. Just as a father begets children who reflect who he is, the divine Father begets mercies that reflect him. There is a family resemblance between the Father and mercy. . . . To speak of God the Father as "the Father of mercies" is to say that he is the one who multiplies compassionate mercies to his needful, wayward, messy, fallen, wandering people. . . . As you consider the Father's heart for you, remember that he is the Father of mercies. He is not cautious in his tenderness toward you. He multiplies mercies matched to your every need, and there is nothing he would rather do.

DANE ORTLUND

15 His "Natural" Work and His "Strange" Work

He does not afflict from his heart
  or grieve the children of men.

LAMENTATIONS 3:33

When he [God] comes to show mercy, to manifest that it is his nature and disposition, it is said that he does it with his whole heart. There is nothing at all in him that is against it. The act itself pleases him for itself. There is no reluctance in him. . . . Therefore acts of justice are called his "strange work" and his "strange act" in Isaiah 28:21 [KJV]. But when he comes to show mercy, he rejoices over them, to do them good, with his whole heart and with his whole soul.

THOMAS GOODWIN

Here in Lamentations, the Bible is taking us deep into God himself. The one who rules and ordains all things brings affliction into our lives with a certain divine reluctance. He is not reluctant about the ultimate good that is going to be brought about through that pain; that indeed is why he is doing it. But something recoils within him in sending that affliction. The pain itself does not reflect his heart. He is not a platonic force pulling heaven's levers and pulleys in a way that is detached from the real pain and anguish we feel at his hand. He is—if I can put it this way without questioning his divine perfections—conflicted within himself when he sends affliction into our lives. God is indeed punishing Israel for their waywardness as the Babylonians sweep through the city. He is sending what they deserve. But his deepest heart is their merciful restoration.

DANE ORTLUND

16   The Lord, the Lord

*The Lord passed before him and proclaimed, "The Lord, the Lord, a God
merciful and gracious, slow to anger, and abounding in steadfast love and faith-
fulness, keeping steadfast love for thousands, forgiving iniquity and transgression
and sin, but who will by no means clear the guilty, visiting the iniquity of the
fathers on the children and the children's children, to the third and the fourth
generation."*

EXODUS 34:6–7

When [God] solemnly declared his nature by his name to the full, that we
might know and fear him, he does it by an enumeration of those properties
which may convince us of his compassionateness and forbearance, and not
till the close of all makes any mention of his severity, as that which he will
not exercise towards any but such as by whom his compassion is despised.

JOHN OWEN

When we speak of God's glory, we are speaking of who God is, what he is
like, his distinctive resplendence, what makes God *God*. And when God
himself sets the terms on what his glory is, he surprises us into wonder.
Our deepest instincts expect him to be thundering, gavel swinging, judg-
ment relishing. We expect the bent of God's heart to be retribution to our
waywardness. And then Exodus 34 taps us on the shoulder and stops us in
our tracks. The bent of God's heart is mercy. His glory is his goodness. . . .
Yes, our sins will be passed down to our children and grandchildren. But
God's goodness will be passed down in a way that inexorably swallows up
all our sins. His mercies travel down a thousand generations, far eclipsing
the third or fourth generation.

DANE ORTLUND

17　His Ways Are Not Our Ways

Let the wicked forsake his way,
*   and the unrighteous man his thoughts;*
let him return to the LORD, that he may have compassion on him,
*   and to our God, for he will abundantly pardon.*
For my thoughts are not your thoughts,
*   neither are your ways my ways, declares the LORD.*
For as the heavens are higher than the earth,
*   so are my ways higher than your ways*
*   and my thoughts than your thoughts.*

ISAIAH 55:7–9

Men are wont to judge and measure God from themselves; for their hearts are moved by angry passions, and are very difficult to be appeased; and therefore they think that they cannot be reconciled to God, when they have once offended him. But the Lord shows that he is far from resembling men.

JOHN CALVIN

God's heart of compassion confounds our intuitive predilections about how he loves to respond to his people if they would but dump in his lap the ruin and wreckage of their lives. He isn't like you. Even the most intense of human love is but the faintest echo of heaven's cascading abundance. His heartful thoughts for you outstrip what you can conceive. He intends to restore you into the radiant resplendence for which you were created. And that is dependent not on you keeping yourself clean but on you taking your mess to him. He doesn't limit himself to working with the unspoiled parts of us that remain after a lifetime of sinning. His power runs so deep that he is able to redeem the very worst parts of our past into the most radiant parts of our future. But we need to take those dark miseries to him.

DANE ORTLUND

18   Yearning Bowels

Is Ephraim [Israel] my dear son?
   Is he my darling child?
For as often as I speak against him,
   I do remember him still.
Therefore my heart yearns for him;
   I will surely have mercy on him,
                        declares the LORD.

JEREMIAH 31:20

There is comfort concerning such infirmities, in that your very sins move him to pity more than to anger. . . . Christ takes part with you, and is far from being provoked against you, as all his anger is turned upon your sin to ruin it; yea, his pity is increased the more towards you, even as the heart of a father is to a child that has some loathsome disease, or as one is to a member of his body that has leprosy, he hates not the member, for it is his flesh, but the disease, and that provokes him to pity the part affected the more. What shall not make for us, when our sins, that are both against Christ and us, shall be turned as motives to him to pity us the more?

THOMAS GOODWIN

Some of us separate out our sins from our sufferings. We are culpable for our sins, after all, whereas our suffering (much of it anyway) is simply what befalls us in this world ruined by the fall. So we tend to have greater difficulty expecting God's gentle compassion toward our sins in the same way as toward our sufferings. Surely his heart flows more freely when I am sinned against than when I myself sin? But observe Goodwin's logic. If the intensity of love maps onto the intensity of misery in the one beloved, and if our greatest misery is our sinfulness, then God's most intense love flows down to us in our sinfulness.

DANE ORTLUND

19　Rich in Mercy

But God, being rich in mercy, because of the great love with which he loved us . . .

EPHESIANS 2:4

He is rich unto all; that is, he is infinite, overflowing in goodness, he is good to a profuseness, he is good to the pouring forth of riches, he is good to an abundance.

THOMAS GOODWIN

Verses 1 through 3 [of Ephesians 2] tell us why we needed saving: we were spiritually dead. Verses 5 and 6 tell us what the saving was: God made us alive. But it's verse 4, right in the middle, that tells us why God saved us. Verses 1–3 are the problem; verses 5–6 are the solution; and verse 4 is the reason God actually went about fixing the problem rather than leaving us where we were. And what is that reason? God is not poor in mercy. He is rich in mercy. Nowhere else in the Bible is God described as rich in anything. The only thing he is called *rich* in is: mercy. What does this mean? It means that God is something other than what we naturally believe him to be. It means the Christian life is a lifelong shedding of tepid thoughts of the goodness of God. In his justice, God is exacting; in his mercy, God is overflowing. . . . God is rich in mercy. He doesn't withhold mercy from some kinds of sinners while extending it to others. Because mercy is who he is—"*being* rich in mercy"—his heart gushes forth mercy to sinners one and all. His mercy overcomes even the deadness of our souls and the hollowed-out, zombie-like existence that we are all naturally born into.

DANE ORTLUND

20 Our Law-ish Hearts, His Lavish Heart

I have been crucified with Christ. It is no longer I who live, but Christ who lives in me. And the life I now live in the flesh I live by faith in the Son of God, who loved me and gave himself for me.

GALATIANS 2:20

Are not you amazed sometimes that you should have so much as a hope, that, poor and needy as you are, the Lord thinks of you? But let not all you feel discourage you. For if our Physician is almighty, our disease cannot be desperate and if He casts none out that come to Him, why should you fear? Our sins are many, but His mercies are more: our sins are great, but His righteousness is greater: we are weak, but He is power. Most of our complaints are owing to unbelief, and the remainder of a legal spirit [works righteousness or legalism, the inveterate yet subtle proclivity to seek to leverage Christ's favor with our behavior].

JOHN NEWTON

There are two ways to live the Christian life. You can live it either *for* the heart of Christ or *from* the heart of Christ. You can live for the smile of God or from it. For a new identity as a son or daughter of God or from it. For your union with Christ or from it. The battle of the Christian life is to bring your own heart into alignment with Christ's, that is, getting up each morning and replacing your natural orphan mind-set with a mind-set of full and free adoption into the family of God through the work of Christ your older brother, who loved you and gave himself for you out of the overflowing fullness of his gracious heart.

DANE ORTLUND

21   He Loved Us Then;
He'll Love Us Now

Since, therefore, we have now been justified by his blood, much more shall we be saved by him from the wrath of God. For if while we were enemies we were reconciled to God by the death of his Son, much more, now that we are reconciled, shall we be saved by his life. More than that, we also rejoice in God through our Lord Jesus Christ, through whom we have now received reconciliation.

ROMANS 5:9–11

As God did not at first choose you because you were high, he will not now forsake you because you are low.

JOHN FLAVEL

What's the ultimate point Paul is driving at in Romans 5:6–11? Not God's past work, mainly. Paul's deepest burden is our present security, given that past work. He raises Christ's past work to drive home this point: if God did that back then, when you were so screwy and had zero interest in him, then what are you worried about now? The central burden of verses 6 through 11 is captured in the "since" of verse 9: "*Since*, therefore, we have now been justified by his blood"—and now we hear Paul's driving concern—"much more shall we be saved by him from the wrath of God." . . . The language of being "saved" in verses 9 and 10 looks ahead to final salvation, referring not to the moment of conversion in this life but entrance into the presence of God in the next. Paul is saying that it is impossible to be truly justified at conversion without God looking after us right into heaven. Conversion isn't a fresh start. Conversion, authentic regeneration, is the invincibilizing of our future.

DANE ORTLUND

22 To the End

Having loved his own who were in the world, he loved them to the end.

JOHN 13:1

Love in Christ decays not, nor can be tempted so to do by anything that happens, or that shall happen hereafter, in the object so beloved. . . . Love in him is essential to his being. God is love; Christ is God; therefore Christ is love, *love naturally*. He may as well cease to be, as cease to love. . . . Love from Christ requires no taking beauteousness in the object to be beloved. It can act of and from itself, without all such kind of dependencies. The Lord Jesus sets his heart to love them.

JOHN BUNYAN

The heart of Christ for sinners and sufferers does not flash with tenderness occasionally or temporarily, sputtering out over time. Gentleness and low-liness of heart is who Christ is steadily, consistently, everlastingly, when all loveliness in us has withered. How do we know? We know because of what John 13:1 says, which the final few chapters of all four Gospel accounts narrate: Jesus came to the cliff of the cross and didn't change his mind. He walked over the edge. . . . In going to the cross, Jesus did not retain something for himself, the way we tend to do when we seek to love others sacrificially. He does not love like us. We love until we are betrayed. Jesus continued to the cross despite betrayal. We love until we are forsaken. Jesus loved through forsakenness. We love up to a limit. Jesus loves to the end.

DANE ORTLUND

23 Buried in His Heart Forevermore

God . . . made us alive together with Christ . . . and raised us up with him and seated us with him in the heavenly places in Christ Jesus, so that in the coming ages he might show the immeasurable riches of his grace in kindness toward us.

EPHESIANS 2:4–7

The creation of the world seems to have been especially for this end, that the eternal Son of God might obtain a spouse, towards whom he might fully exercise the infinite benevolence of his nature, and to whom he might, as it were, open and pour forth all that immense fountain of condescension, love, and grace that was in his heart, and that in this way God might be glorified.

JONATHAN EDWARDS

Ephesians 2:7 is telling you that your death is not an end but a beginning. Not a wall, but a door. Not an exit, but an entrance. The point of all human history and eternity itself is to show what cannot be fully shown. To demonstrate what cannot be adequately demonstrated. In the coming age we will descend ever deeper into God's grace in kindness, into his very heart, and the more we understand of it, the more we will see it to be beyond understanding. It is immeasurable. For those not in Christ, this life is the best it will ever get. For those in Christ, for whom Ephesians 2:7 is the eternal vista just around the next bend in the road, this life is the worst it will ever get.

DANE ORTLUND